ART REVOLUTIONS
IMPRESSIONISM,

Linda Bolton

PETER BEDRICK BOOKS
NTC/Contemporary Publishing Group
NEW YORK

This American edition published 2000 by Peter Bedrick Books,
a division of NTC/Contemporary Publishing Group, Inc.,
4255 West Touhy Avenue, Lincolnwood (Chicago),
Illinois 60646-1975 U.S.A.

First published in Great Britain in 2000 by Belitha Press Limited,
London House. Great Eastern Wharf, Parkgate Road, London SW11 4NQ

Editor Susie Brooks
Designer Helen James
Picture Researcher Diana Morris
Educational Consultant Hester Collicutt
Consultants for US Edition Nathaniel Harris, Ruth Nason

Printed in China

International Standard Book Number: 0-87226-611-7

Library of Congress Cataloging-in-Publication data
is available from the United States Library of Congress.

00 01 02 03   15 14 13 12 11 10 9 8 7 6 5 4 3 2 1

Picture Credits:

Front cover: Pierre Auguste Renoir, Boating Party Lunch, 1881. Phillips Collection, Washington. Photo Edward Owen/Bridgeman Art Library. 1: Pierre Auguste Renoir, The Swing, 1876. Musée d'Orsay, Paris. Photo Giraudon/Bridgeman Art Library. 4: Claude Monet, Impression, Sunrise, 1872. Musée Marmottan, Paris. Photo Peter Willi/Bridgeman Art Library, © DACS 2000. 5: J. M. W. Turner, Rain, Steam, and Speed, 1844. National Gallery, London. Photo Erich Lessing/AKG London. 6: Pierre Auguste Renoir, La Loge, 1874. Courtauld Institute Galleries, London. Photo Bridgeman Art Library. 7t: Edouard Manet, The Rue Mosnier with Pavers, 1878. Private Collection. Photo Bridgeman Art Library. 7b: Claude Monet, Gare Saint-Lazare, 1877. Musée d'Orsay, Paris. Photo Bulloz/Bridgeman Art Library, © DACS 2000. 8: Claude Monet, Wild Poppies, 1873. Musée d'Orsay, Paris. Photo Peter Willi/Bridgeman Art Library, © DACS 2000. 9t: Claude Monet, The Magpie, 1868–69. Musée d'Orsay, Paris. Photo Peter Willi/Bridgeman Art Library, © DACS 2000. 9b: Claude Monet, Rue Montorgueil, 1878. Musée d'Orsay, Paris. Photo Bulloz/Bridgeman Art Library, © DACS 2000. 10: Pierre Auguste Renoir, Ball at the Moulin de la Galette, 1876. Musée d'Orsay, Paris. Photo Giraudon/Bridgeman Art Library. 11t: Pierre Auguste Renoir, Boating Party Luncheon, 1881. Phillips Collection, Washington. Photo Edward Owen/Bridgeman Art Library. 11b: Pierre Auguste Renoir, The Swing, 1876. Musée d'Orsay, Paris. Photo Giraudon/Bridgeman Art Library. 12: Camille Pissarro, Entrance to Village of Voisins, 1872. Musée d'Orsay, Paris. Photo Giraudon/Bridgeman Art Library. 13t: Camille Pissarro, Boulevard Montmartre at Night, 1897. National Gallery, London. Photo Bridgeman Art Library. 13b: Camille Pissarro, Coach at Louveciennes, 1870. Musée d'Orsay, Paris. Photo Bridgeman Art Library. 14: Alfred Sisley, Canal at St. Martin, Paris, 1872. Musée d'Orsay, Paris. Photo Erich Lessing/AKG London. 15t: Alfred Sisley, Rue de la Chaussée, Argenteuil, 1872. Musée d'Orsay, Paris. Photo Giraudon/ Bridgeman Art Library. 15b: Alfred Sisley, Barge During Floods, Port Marly, 1876. Musée d'Orsay, Paris. Photo Erich Lessing/ AKG London. 16: Edouard Manet, The Balcony, 1869. Musée d'Orsay, Paris. Photo Erich Lessing/AKG London. 17t: Edouard Manet, Bar at the Folies-Bergère, 1882. Courtauld Insititute Galleries, London. Photo Bridgeman Art Library. 17b: Edouard Manet, Argenteuil, Monet's Studio Boat, 1874. Neue Pinakothek, Munich. Photo Bridgeman Art Library. 18: Berthe Morisot, The Cradle, 1872. Musée d'Orsay, Paris. Photo Peter Willi/ Bridgeman Art Library. 19: Berthe Morisot, In the Dining Room, 1886. National Gallery of Art, Washington. Photo Bridgeman Art Library. 20: Edgar Degas, Café Concert, 1876–77. Musée des Beaux Arts, Lyons. Photo Giraudon/ Bridgeman Art Library. 21t: Edgar Degas, L'Étoile, 1875–76. Musée d'Orsay, Paris. Photo Erich Lessing/AKG London. 21b: Edgar Degas, Miss La La, 1879. National Gallery, London. Photo Bridgeman Art Library. 22: Mary Cassatt, In the Loge, 1882. National Gallery of Art, Washington. Photo Bridgeman Art Library. 23: Mary Cassatt, The Cup of Tea, 1879. Metropolitan Museum of Art, Collection of James Stillman. Gift of Dr. Ernest G. Stillman, 1922. Photograph © 1998 Metropolitan Museum of Art. 24: Gustave Caillebotte, Paris in the Rain, 1877. Art Institute of Chicago. Photo Erich Lessing/AKG London. 25t: Gustave Caillebotte, Floorplaners, 1875. Musée d'Orsay, Paris. Photo Lauros-Giraudon/Bridgeman Art Library. 25b: Gustave Caillebotte, Le Pont de l'Europe, 1876. Petit Palais, Geneva. Photo Bridgeman Art Library. 26: Vincent Van Gogh, Moulin de la Galette, Montmartre, 1886. Glasgow Art Gallery & Museum. Photo Bridgeman Art Library. 27: Vincent Van Gogh, Restaurant de la Sirène, Asnières, 1878. Musée d'Orsay, Paris. Photo Peter Willi/ Bridgeman Art Library. 28t: James McNeill Whistler, Nocturne in Blue and Gold, 1865. Tate Gallery, London. Photo Erich Lessing/AKG London. 28b: Paul Gauguin, Rue Carcel Covered in Snow, 1883. Ny Carlsberg Glyptothek, Copenhagen. Photo Erich Lessing/AKG London. 29t: Paul Cézanne, Tall Trees at the Jas de Bouffan, 1883. Courtauld Institute Galleries, London. Photo Bridgeman Art Library. 29b: Georges Seurat, Sunday Afternoon on the Island of La Grande Jatte, 1884–86. Art Institute of Chicago. Photo Bridgeman Art Library.

CONTENTS

Useful words are explained on page 30.

IMPRESSIONIST SHOCKS

In 1874 a group of artists, now known as the Impressionists, put on an exhibition of their paintings in Paris. When the public and critics saw them, some were angry and others laughed. Leading Impressionists such as Monet, Renoir, and Pissarro were hailed as great artists only after a long struggle.

The Impressionists took their subjects from the life of their own time, which meant painting city scenes and landscapes, showing people of all classes strolling or enjoying themselves.

Their pictures were bright and atmospheric and dashingly painted. Nowadays they are immensely popular and famous, but in 1874 they caused a scandal because they broke away from tradition.

Bright, modern works were seldom allowed into the official exhibition of French art, known as the Salon. The Salon showed what is now called academic art – large pictures of historical and other "serious" subjects, painted in rather dark colors. Most people accepted that this was how good art should look. Impressionist paintings seemed to have the wrong subjects and also to be painted in the wrong way.

Instead of working in their studios, the Impressionists often painted outdoors (in French, *plein-air*), trying to capture momentary effects of light and atmosphere. The painters had to work fast, using big brushstrokes and dabs of pure color to build up figures without putting in hard outlines or smoothing down the surface. The technique, known as broken brushwork, created a lively atmosphere. A recent invention, tubes of ready-made paint, made it easier to work on the move.

J.M.W. TURNER
Rain, Steam, and Speed

1844, oil paint on canvas

Over thirty years before the Impressionists, the British artist Turner was painting the changing effects of nature in his own style. The picture above shows a steam train roaring through the rain and mist. Turner's work was seen by Monet and Pissarro when they were staying in London, and it may have influenced their work. They had fled to England for a while during the Franco-Prussian War of 1870–71, in which France was disastrously defeated. The war affected all the Impressionists.

CLAUDE MONET
Impression, Sunrise

1872, oil paint on canvas

This painting gave the new art movement its name. At the 1874 exhibition, the art critic Louis Leroy noticed the word "impression" in the title of Monet's painting and wrote, mockingly, that all the artists on show were impressionists. He meant that their work was sketchy and unfinished. But from then on, the artists defiantly used the word to describe themselves.

The 1874 Impressionist exhibition took place in Paris, and seven more Impressionist exhibitions were held there between 1876 and 1886. The city was changing fast during this period. Until 1853, most of Paris had consisted of narrow old streets without modern amenities. Then the Emperor Napoleon III put Baron Haussmann in charge. Under Haussmann, old houses were knocked down to build splendid, wide, tree-lined boulevards and modern places of work and entertainment. The fashionable new city was alive with cafés and theaters. The cafés were important as places where writers and artists – including the Impressionists – met and formed groups to launch new ideas. All this helped make Paris a great art center.

PIERRE AUGUSTE RENOIR
La Loge

1874, oil paint on canvas

"La loge" is French, meaning "the box." Boxes are the grandest places to sit in a theater, and the couple here are beautifully dressed. Renoir did not paint them in stiff poses as if for a portrait, but acting naturally. The man uses his opera glasses to survey the audience, while the woman is thoughtfully aware that people are staring at her. This is one of the seven works shown by Renoir at the 1874 exhibition.

EDOUARD MANET

The Rue Mosnier
with Pavers

1878, oil paint on canvas

This is a scene that Manet saw from his studio window. The painting records everyday events. Carriages pass in the street and pavers work on the road surface, their forms and movements indicated by a few bold brushstrokes.

CLAUDE MONET

The Gare Saint-Lazare

1877, oil paint on canvas

Railroad stations were symbols of the modern age of steam. Monet chose the Gare Saint-Lazare in Paris as the subject for a series of paintings. The station master was so flattered that he ordered a train driver to release a puff of engine steam, especially for Monet to paint. Monet generally chose scenes like this one, in which atmospheric conditions made objects appear to blend into one another.

CLAUDE MONET
1840–1926

"The father of Impressionism."

Monet was one of the leading Impressionists. He grew up in Normandy, where he was encouraged to paint outside by the artist Eugène Boudin. When Monet moved to Paris to study art, he persuaded others to work in the open air.

Monet moved back to Normandy later in his life. Wherever he lived, he painted the world around him, often recording the same scene in different lights and colors. As he grew old, his favorite subject became his water garden at Giverny.

Wild Poppies
1873, oil paint on canvas

As a young artist, Monet did not have much money. Paris was an expensive city, so he moved to Argenteuil, on the outskirts, to avoid high rents and find new subjects to paint. Fellow Impressionists Renoir, Sisley, Pissarro, and Manet often joined him there. Here Monet has painted his wife Camille and their son Jean, walking in a field of poppies. He aimed to capture the scene as it looked at one moment. The colors are warm and bright – we can almost feel the heat of the sun shining through the drifting clouds and hear the breeze whispering in the long grass.

COMBINING COLORS
Colors that are opposite each other on this wheel are called complementaries. Together they combine red, yellow, and blue. For example, purple (red plus blue) is the complementary of yellow. The Impressionists combined colors in ways that made their pictures glow.

The Magpie
1869, oil paint
on canvas

Here Monet makes us feel the crisp, cold air of a bright winter morning. He has created a dazzling effect by carefully choosing his colors. The shadows are not made up of blacks and grays (the shades that traditional artists would have used), but of blues and mauves. These contrast with tints of yellow and pink in the brilliant white patches of sunlit snow. Seen close up, Monet's canvas is a mass of thick, multicolored paintwork. Like many Impressionist works, it is best viewed from a distance: then the brushstrokes merge and the picture becomes clear.

Rue Montorgueil, Paris
1878, oil paint on canvas

In the late 1860s, the Impressionists started to paint views of Paris. Monet painted this busy scene on a national holiday in June. The bright colors evoke the noise and excitement of the sunny summer festival. Monet has avoided solid outlines and fussy details. His lively brushwork gives the effect of movement. Sketchy strokes of red, white, and blue paint represent thousands of flapping French flags. The blurred forms swarming below them are people.

PIERRE AUGUSTE RENOIR
1841–1919

"The artist with the rainbow palette."

Pierre Auguste Renoir, son of a tailor and one of five children, enjoyed a happy working-class childhood in Paris. He began his artistic career as a porcelain decorator, making pictures on cups and plates. Afterward he trained as a painter, sharing a studio with his friend Monet.

Renoir loved to paint people enjoying themselves – groups of friends dining and dancing in bright surroundings, or couples chatting in shady parks. Many of his works capture the effect of sunlight shining through leaves and falling on people's clothes. His paintings are full of life.

Ball at the Moulin de la Galette
1876, oil paint on canvas

The Moulin de la Galette was an old mill in Paris which had been turned into a dance hall. In the summer, dances were held in the courtyard outside. Renoir went there to paint, and here we see a group of his friends, talking and dancing with local girls. The arrangement of so many figures in one painting is remarkable. It is unlikely that Renoir painted this large canvas on the spot. He probably made sketches there, to work from back in his studio.

Boating Party Luncheon

1881, oil paint on canvas

Renoir painted this merry midday scene at Bougival, a picturesque spot on the River Seine. Many Parisians held boating parties there in the summer. This group is finishing lunch, enjoying each other's company around tables full of bottles, glasses, and fruit. Renoir has painted the figures in relaxed positions. They do not look as if they are posing. The glowing light makes us feel warm, as if we are there too.

COLORED LIGHT

Renoir applied blobs of color among patches of white to achieve different light effects. For example, a dab of red in the middle of a white patch created a delicate green tinge. This happens because green is the complementary of red.

The Swing

1876, oil paint on canvas

In this painting, touches of color create a dappled effect which is typical of Renoir's outdoor scenes. Sunlight shimmering through the leaves of the trees patterns the figures and the ground with spots of light and shadow. The little girl on the left stands partly in the sunlight, watching the adults chatting in the shade. Her form and features are simplified, as if hard to see in the sun.

CAMILLE PISSARRO 1830–1903

"It is good to draw everything..."

Camille Pissarro was born in the Virgin Islands, in the Caribbean, but was sent to school in Paris. Later he trained there as a painter, befriending the other Impressionists even though he was several years older than them.

Pissarro was the only artist to exhibit in all eight Impressionist shows. He was also a great teacher, working with many younger artists from Cassatt to Cézanne. His emphasis on drawing shows in the structure and perspective of the scenes here.

Entrance to Village of Voisins, Yvelines

1872, oil paint on canvas

One of Pissarro's favorite subjects was a road – especially in the country. This is the approach to Voisins, a village that he knew well. We can imagine him putting up his easel at the side of the road to paint what he saw. The air seems fresh and clear. Tall, spindly trees cast long shadows across the dusty track and green grass roadside. We feel as if we are there on a calm spring morning, hearing singing birds and the clip-clop of the horse's hoofs.

Boulevard Montmartre at Night
1897, oil paint on canvas

Toward the end of his life, Pissarro gave up painting outdoors, because his eyesight was beginning to fail, and instead he painted many views from windows in Paris. He painted this nighttime scene from an apartment overlooking the Boulevard Montmartre. We see the artificial light from lampposts, buildings, and horse-drawn carriages reflected by the wet road and sidewalks. Pissarro's brushstrokes follow the diagonal skyline, emphasizing the sweep of the road into the distance. People are sketched in with dashes of paint, giving the impression that the figures are moving.

CHANGE OF SCENE
Like most of the Impressionist painters, Pissarro was interested in the way a view looked different, depending on the time of day and the weather. So he started to paint the same scene in various conditions, including thirteen views of the boulevard above.

Coach at Louveciennes
1870, oil paint on canvas

The town of Louveciennes was a few miles outside Paris. Pissarro moved there to live more cheaply but still be within easy reach of the city. Monet and Renoir lived nearby, and all three often saw friends in Paris. They probably traveled in a horse-drawn coach such as the one in this painting, shown pausing on a rainy street. Pissarro's broken brushwork creates the impression of evening light glistening on wet cobblestones. The dazzling pinks and whites give a sense of light filtered through the clouds. The atmosphere is warm, damp, and calm.

ALFRED SISLEY 1839–1899

Alfred Sisley was born in Paris to English parents. At the age of eighteen he was sent to London for a business career, but, eager to be an artist, he soon returned to France. The Sisley family lost their money as a result of the Franco-Prussian War, and Alfred had to try to sell his work to make a living. Unlike other Impressionists, he never gave up the style. But he was the least-known artist of the group, and never made much money, as Monet and Renoir eventually did. Sisley's paintings are everyday views of quiet French villages and simple riverside scenery.

Canal at St. Martin, Paris

1872, oil paint on canvas

This quiet canal was one of the spots in Paris that Sisley liked to paint. We feel as if we are looking at the water from a bridge, comfortably distant from the action on the far bank. The overwhelming effect is of calm sky and water – elements which Sisley loved to paint. He tried to create the impression of gently drifting clouds above rippling water. Light from the blue sky glints on the river's surface, creating reflections. Sisley varies his brushstrokes to give the effect of movement. There is also a strong sense of space, which makes us feel the fresh air of this sunny day.

WATER WATCH
Broken brushstrokes are a particularly effective way of painting reflections on water. Sisley and Monet used long horizontal strokes to represent ripples.

Rue de la Chaussée, Argenteuil
1872, oil on canvas

Sisley often painted at Argenteuil, either on his own or with his Impressionist friends. Here the buildings are bathed in the golden sunlight of a summer evening. It is a peaceful scene in which we enjoy the impression of being in a wide open space, with a small number of people going quietly about their business. Sisley probably set up his easel in the square to make this painting. We feel we are standing in the shade, looking down a street that disappears into a quaint jumble of houses.

Barge During Floods, Port Marly
1876, oil paint on canvas

Sisley was known as the poet of the riverbanks. He loved to paint water in every season and weather condition. In 1876 the banks of the River Seine burst at Port Marly, where Sisley was living. He painted three pictures of the floods. In this one, two men in a boat are punting in the flood waters. There is a sense of calm after a storm, of clear air after pouring rain. The light wind-blown clouds, blue sky, and the inn are reflected in the gently rippling water. Cool, fresh colors are laid down in broad strokes.

EDOUARD MANET   1832–1883

Edouard Manet did not show his work in any of the Impressionist exhibitions, but he did play an important part in the movement. He was leader of *la bande à Manet,* or Manet's gang – a group who met regularly in cafés to talk about painting.

The younger artists were interested in Manet's ideas and painting techniques, and their ideas influenced him. Manet broke with tradition in considering it important to paint modern life. It is said that he paved the way for modern art.

The Balcony

1869, oil paint on canvas

Here we see a group of Manet's friends, posing on the balcony of a Paris apartment. The figure seated on the left is Berthe Morisot. She was Manet's pupil and model, and became a famous Impressionist herself. Manet was very fond of Morisot. He seems to have taken more care in painting her than the other woman, violinist Fanny Claus, and the man, landscape artist Antoine Guillemet. The figures seem to be isolated from one another, all gazing out in different directions at some spectacle in the street. We feel as if we are looking at them from the balcony of a building across the way. Do they know they are being watched?

MAKE IT MODERN
Modern life was Manet's theme. He shocked critics when he painted nudes as modern young women instead of as goddesses.

Bar at the Folies-Bergère
1882, oil paint on canvas

The people reflected in the mirror behind the barmaid went to the Folies-Bergère to drink, chat, and be seen. Few of them seem to notice the trapeze artist, whose legs are dangling at the top left of the painting. The placid barmaid looks as if she is thinking about something else, but the reflection on the right shows she is serving a customer. Manet used "real" and mirror images, and near and distant objects, to vary the picture and make it hum with life.

Manet's friend Claude Monet loved painting water, so he converted a boat into a studio! Another friend and painter, Gustave Caillebotte, designed it for him. It had a cabin in which to store equipment, and a striped canopy to keep off the rain or sun. Here Manet has painted Monet working on his boat at Argenteuil. His wife Camille is with him. In the background are smoky factory chimneys, symbols of the modern city. Is Monet painting them too? Manet creates the effect of light reflected on water by laying down dabs of bright paint among patches of deeper color. His sketchy brushwork makes a breezy scene.

Monet in his Studio Boat, Argenteuil
1874, oil paint on canvas

BERTHE MORISOT 1841–1895

"The one real Impressionist."

Berthe Morisot came from a wealthy family. She and her sister trained as painters in Paris, where Berthe met Manet in 1868. She often modeled for him. In 1874 she married his brother, Eugène.

Morisot exhibited in seven of the eight Impressionist shows. She and Eugène had plenty of money, so they were able to help fund the 1886 exhibition. Morisot painted everyday family scenes in simple yet elegant interiors. She applied her paint freely, with a very sure touch. Her brushstrokes are very light, feathery, and delicate.

The Cradle
1872, oil paint on canvas

Here we see a simple scene of a mother tenderly rocking her baby's cradle. The woman is Berthe's sister, Edma. Her dark hair and dress are framed by the white curtain in the window. The whiteness of the curtain is muted by soft blues and pale orange tones, which push it into the background. The white of the fabric draped over the cradle is brighter. Morisot has used dazzling pinks and golds to give the impression of light shimmering on delicate material. The different textures in the painting and the transparency of the draped fabrics are brilliantly conveyed

In the Dining Room

1886, oil paint on canvas

This painting shows Morisot's maid in the dining room of her house. It is painted in a sketchy way, making us feel that it was done on the spot. The maid seems to be pausing for a second, as if unexpectedly interrupted from her work to allow a photograph to be taken. The sweeping streaks of paint give the impression that, before she stopped, the maid was bustling around the room. The little dog is also captured in mid-movement. Morisot uses delicate touches of white paint to create the effect of light blazing through the window and glinting on the maid's hair, shoulder, arm, hand, and apron. She makes us feel the warmth and comfort of this sunny room.

EDGAR DEGAS 1834–1917

"Painter of the stage."

Edgar Degas did not consider himself an Impressionist, but he often showed his paintings and sculptures in the group exhibitions. Although he studied academic art, Degas's theme was modern life and his approach revolutionary.

Degas chose to paint horse-racing scenes, cafés, and ballet, theater, and circus performers. His interest was in showing people and movement, and the effect of artificial light indoors. Unlike the Impressionists, he hated *plein-air* painting.

Café Concert at Les Ambassadeurs

1876–77, pastel over monotype

Café concerts were a popular kind of entertainment in Impressionist times. People came to enjoy a show while having a drink with friends. Here Degas recreates the lively atmosphere of an evening performance. The unusual viewpoint makes us feel as if we are sitting in the darkness of the audience, looking down at a bright stage. Lights from below glint on the singers' faces and costumes. The red, blue, and yellow dresses catch our eye, drawing attention to the action on the stage. Before working with the Impressionists, Degas drew using line – he did not think much about color. But by working in pastel he could draw and use color at the same time.

L'Étoile (The Star)
1875–76, pastel over monotype

Degas compared his art to ballet. Both he and the dancer worked very hard to produce something which looked effortless. Here we see a ballet dancer taking a graceful bow. The unusual angle makes us feel as if we are looking at her from a box high above the left of the stage. We also glimpse the stage manager and some dancers in the wings. Degas creates the impression of a light-footed ballerina in her delicate costume, by using soft pastel colors. Shimmering white touches give the effect of a spotlight shining on the stage.

Miss La La
1879, oil paint on canvas

Miss La La was a performer with the Fernando Circus, which Degas went to see daily while it was in Paris. She was famous for holding a cannon on a chain between her teeth, while hanging by her legs from a trapeze. During the show, the cannon was fired to prove that it was real and to add drama. Degas was a great admirer of the daring Miss La La. Here we see her close to the roof of the Big Top, dangling by her teeth. It is a tense moment. We can almost hear the drum roll as she prepares to spin to the ground.

A NEW TECHNIQUE
Before Degas, figures and objects in most paintings were placed squarely inside the frame. Degas often cut them off (like the round light, page 20), giving a lively snapshot effect.

MARY CASSATT 1844–1926

"The American Impressionist."

Mary Cassatt was introduced to the other Impressionists by her close friend, the painter Edgar Degas. The daughter of an American banker, she studied in Philadelphia, then in Paris, and later in Italy and Spain.

Cassatt often posed for Degas, as Morisot did for Manet. She was wealthy enough to buy many Impressionist works, as well as creating her own. Cassatt painted the everyday life and people she knew – at home, at the theater, and at the opera.

In the Loge
1882, oil paint on canvas

Here we see two girls seated in a box at the theater. Behind them is a mirror reflecting the wider scene. The painting reminds us of Renoir's *La Loge* (page 6), but unlike the figures in this earlier work, Cassatt's girls look self-conscious, as if this is their first outing. One raises her fan to her face, as if she is hiding from view. The curve of the fan makes part of a circle that continues through the slope of the other girl's shoulder and the little bunch of flowers in her lap. This composition brings the figures together. Cassatt uses soft colors and broad brushstrokes to increase the intimate feeling.

The Cup of Tea

1879, oil paint on canvas

Cassatt often painted members of her family, and in particular her sister, Lydia. Here Lydia sits holding a cup of tea. We see her in close-up, as if from a nearby chair. Taking tea was part of the everyday social routine for ladies in Cassatt's circle. It was an excuse to meet and entertain friends in the privacy of each other's homes. Lydia's gloves and bonnet suggest that she is not in her own home, but out on a visit. The soft folds and varied textures of her outfit are captured by broad, carefully placed brushstrokes. Lydia smiles as if she is enjoying the company of someone we cannot see. The painting has a rosy glow which makes us feel warm and relaxed.

BACK HOME
Impressionist art was hardly known in the USA until Mary Cassatt encouraged her brother and wealthy friends to collect it. The first Impressionist exhibition in New York was held in 1886.

GUSTAVE CAILLEBOTTE
1848–1894

"The forgotten man of Impressionism."

Gustave Caillebotte was a marine engineer and painted as a hobby. He had plenty of money, and helped the other Impressionists by buying their work. Many of the paintings now in the Musée d'Orsay, Paris, were owned by him.

Caillebotte did not use the rough, broken brushwork typical of Impressionism. He thought out his pictures in stages, rather than painting them on the spot. But, like the other Impressionists, he chose to portray scenes of modern daily life.

Paris in the Rain 1877, oil paint on canvas

This is a huge painting of an area of Paris that Caillebotte knew well. As he grew up, he had seen it change from a quiet hill with just a few houses on it, to a smart residential center. Caillebotte makes us feel that we are looking at a vast open space. Strong diagonal lines make the buildings zoom away into the distance, while the bold figures in the foreground seem to be walking straight into us. The way in which Caillebotte has cut off the man on the right makes the painting like a snapshot. It is as if we are looking at the scene through a wide-angle camera lens. The Impressionists often used effects they had learned from photography.

Floorplaners

1875, oil paint on canvas

Here we see a Parisian interior with three men planing a varnished wooden floor. This is the kind of scene from everyday life that the Impressionists liked to paint. Caillebotte's interest in light effects is also typical of Impressionism. Here he has shown sunshine pouring in through the window and hitting the floor. Close to the window, the boards shine brightly, but toward the front of the painting the room and figures become very dark. Forms are lit by a few simple highlights. This is the effect that a camera produces when you take a photograph looking toward the sun.

LEFT TO THE NATION

Caillebotte died young and left his wonderful collection of 67 Impressionist paintings to the French nation. Amazingly, only 38 were accepted, and even then the official Academy of Fine Arts protested against them!

Le Pont de l'Europe

1876, oil paint on canvas

This is the big iron bridge over the Saint-Lazare railroad station that Monet often painted. Caillebotte shows a white puff of smoke from a train, rising up into a clear sky. He uses subtle contrasts of yellows and blues to create the impression of light and shade on a sunny day. This is an image of the modern city, with ordinary people passing by. The artist was about 28 years old when he painted this. The figure in the top hat is probably a self-portrait. Our eyes are drawn toward him by the diagonal lines of the bridge, making him the center of attention.

VINCENT VAN GOGH 1853–1890

"Seeking life in color."

Van Gogh was born in Holland. He moved to Paris in 1886, and saw the modern French paintings he had heard about from his brother, Theo, an art dealer in the city. Theo introduced Vincent to many painters, including Pissarro, whose colorful brushwork inspired him.

Younger than the main Impressionists, Van Gogh learned much from them. He used similar broken brushstrokes and painted scenes of everyday life. But over time he developed a somewhat different style, using color to express his emotions. For this reason, he is often called a Post-Impressionist.

Moulin de la Galette, Montmartre

1886, oil paint on canvas

Here we see an old wooden mill, on an unspoiled hilltop in 1880s Paris. The sketchy painting suggests a blustery day. Dashes of red, white, and blue on top of the mill depict a set of French flags fluttering in the breeze. Van Gogh has blurred the edges of the mill's sails to give the impression that they are spinning. Nearby is a raised wooden platform on which some people are shown by simple brushstrokes. Soon, Van Gogh switched to an even brighter Impressionist palette, as in the painting opposite.

Restaurant de la Sirène, Asnières

1887, oil paint on canvas

A FEELING FOR COLOR

Van Gogh believed that color made you feel emotion. Yellow was his favorite – it made him happy. Among his most famous works were a series of sunflower paintings which consisted almost entirely of various shades of yellow. And when he left Paris and went to live in Arles in the south of France, he rented – "the Yellow House"!

Van Gogh was very interested in the experiments which the Impressionists were making with color. Here he has completely abandoned dull browns and grays and used strokes of pure color instead. Like Monet and many other Impressionists, he has contrasted pale blue shadows with bright yellow light. The sky is dazzling in white and yellow, with little touches of blue on the left. The street is painted in the same way, using yellow paint with dabs of blue to suggest faint shadows dappling the ground. We almost feel the hot sunshine beating down on this bright scene.

Many other painters were influenced by the Impressionists' use of bright color and broken brushwork. The paintings here are just a few examples of works that were inspired by this first modern art style.

JAMES McNEILL WHISTLER
Nocturne in Blue and Gold:
Old Battersea Bridge

1865, oil paint on canvas

Whistler (1834–1903) was an American artist who worked in Paris, where he knew the Impressionists. He made this painting after settling in England in 1859. It shows a bridge over the River Thames, in dim evening light, with fireworks being set off in the background.

PAUL GAUGUIN
Rue Carcel Covered in Snow
1883, oil paint on canvas

Like Van Gogh, Gauguin (1848–1903) looked at the Impressionists' paintings and worked in a similar style. His friend Pissarro told him to abandon blacks and use only mixtures of the three primary colors. This painting captures the cold of a snowy morning. The delicate brushwork makes it look like a scene that Pissarro himself might have painted.

PAUL CÉZANNE

Tall Trees at the Jas de Bouffan

1883, oil on canvas

Cézanne (1839-1906) was introduced to *plein-air* painting and the bright Impressionist palette by Pissarro. This painting shows how he separated color into blocks, playing with complementaries to create areas of light and shade. Cézanne's brush-marks are more regular than the sketchy Impressionist strokes, yet he still creates the fleeting effect of windblown leaves. The bright blue between the trees makes us feel the intense heat of a summer sky.

GEORGES SEURAT

Sunday Afternoon on the Island of La Grande Jatte

1884–86, oil paint on canvas

Seurat (1859–91) was very interested in the science of color and how we see it. This painting is made up of millions of dots of pure color, placed close together so that our eyes partially mix them as we look. When he saw this work in the Impressionist show of 1886, the art critic Félix Fénéon called the new style Neo-Impressionism.

academic art Art that followed the principles of the French Academy. The Academy promoted art that was highly finished and pictured historical or mythological events rather than modern scenes.

boulevards Wide avenues in a French city.

broken brushwork Paint applied in irregular patches so that the individual strokes are visible.

canvas A strong fabric on which artists paint. It is usually stretched across a wooden frame and, before any painting is done, lined with a chalky pigment called gesso.

complementary colors Colors that are opposite each other on the color wheel, such as red/green, blue/orange, and yellow/purple.

composition The way a work of art is arranged.

Franco-Prussian War A war that raged between France and Prussia (now part of Germany) from 1870 to 1871. During this time Monet and Pissarro escaped to London.

image A picture or idea.

loge A box in the theater containing the most expensive seats.

metropolis A busy modern city, such as Paris.

monotype A print made by laying paper over a piece of glass or metal which has an image painted onto it in ink.

movement A style or period of art.

muted Softened or dimmed.

Neo-Impressionism A term invented by art critic Félix Fénéon to describe Seurat's style of painting in little dots of pure color. This method is also known as Pointillism or Divisionism.

oil paint A thick paint with a buttery texture, for centuries the most important medium used by artists.

palette A range of colors used.

pastels Colored chalky crayons.

pigment The powdery ingredient that gives paint its color. Early pigments were made from natural materials; modern ones may be chemically based.

plein-air painting Painting an outdoor subject on the spot.

Post-Impressionism A term used to describe art that followed some Impressionist principles and rejected others. Cézanne, Gauguin, Van Gogh, and Seurat are often known as Post-Impressionists.

primary colors Red, yellow, and blue. These colors can be mixed to make every other color, except shades of black and white.

pure color Color that is applied without mixing or blending.

self-portrait An image that an artist makes of him/herself.

studio An artist's indoor workplace.

IMPRESSIONIST TIMES

1830 First passenger steam train.

1839 First photograph produced from negative by Englishman William Fox Talbot. Frenchman Eugène Chevreul publishes first book on complementary color theory.

1840 Invention of oil paint in tubes.

1851 The Emperor Napoleon III takes power and sets out to make Paris a modern metropolis.

1870 Franco-Prussian War breaks out.

1874 First Impressionist exhibition.

1876 Second Impressionist exhibition.

1877 Third Impressionist exhibition.

1879 Fourth Impressionist exhibition. First electric light bulb made in the USA by Thomas Alva Edison.

1880 Fifth Impressionist exhibition. Monet separates from group.

1881 Sixth Impressionist exhibition.

1882 Seventh Impressionist exhibition.

1886 Eighth Impressionist exhibition. Later in year, critic Félix Fénéon declares Impressionism dead.

FURTHER INFORMATION

Galleries to visit
The best places to see original Impressionist works are in Paris, where the movement was born. The **Musée d'Orsay** has the largest collection, much of which was given to the French nation by Gustave Caillebotte. Other examples are housed in the **Orangerie** in the Tuileries Gardens. More of Monet's paintings can be seen at the **Musée Marmottan**. His garden at Giverny, outside Paris, can also be visited during the summer.

In the USA, Impressionist works can be seen at the **Museum of Fine Arts, Boston**; the **Art Institute, Chicago**; the **Philadelphia Museum of Art**; the **Metropolitan Museum of Art** and the **Museum of Modern Art**, in **New York**; and the **National Gallery of Art, Washington, D.C.**

Websites to browse
http://www.artchive.com
http://www.oir.ue.ucf.edu/wm
http://www.cafeguerbois

Books to read
Cézanne, Monet, and *Van Gogh,* from the *Famous Artists* series, Barrons, 1994–95

Degas and the Little Dancer by Laurence Anholt, Barrons, 1996

Impressionism by Jude Welton, DK *Eyewitness Guides,* 1993

Impressionism by Judy Martin, Wayland, 1995

The Impressionists by Francesco Salvi, from the *Masters of Art* series, Peter Bedrick Books, 1994 (also a title on *Van Gogh*)

Visiting Vincent Van Gogh by Caroline Breunesse, Prestel *Adventures in Art* series, 1997 (also a title on *Monet*)

What Makes a Degas a Degas? by Richard Mühlberger, Metropolitan Museum of Art, 1993–95 (also titles on *Cassatt, Monet,* and *Van Gogh*)

INDEX